Adaptation

S0-DYT-156

by Libby Romero

Table of Contents

What are **adaptations**? Why do animals need adaptations? Read this book to learn about adaptations.

Words to Know

adaptations

camouflage

climate

enemies

habitats

migration

prey

protection

survive

See the Glossary on page 30.

3

What Are Adaptations?

Adaptations help animals **survive** in their **habitats**. Animals need food to survive. Adaptations help animals get food.

▲ Long tongues help anteaters get food. Long tongues are an adaptation.

Did You Know?

Plants have adaptations, too. Some adaptations help plants get sunlight. Orchids grow high on trees. The orchids can get sunlight. Growing high on trees is an adaptation.

Animals need **protection** from the **climate** to survive. Adaptations protect animals from the climate.

▲ Whales have a thick layer of fat. The fat protects whales from cold ocean waters.

Did You Know?

Plants have adaptations for climate. This cactus grows in a dry climate. The large stem is full of water. The large stem is an adaptation.

Animals need protection from **enemies** to survive. Adaptations protect animals from their enemies.

▲ **Opossums pretend they are dead. Then enemies do not eat the opossums.**

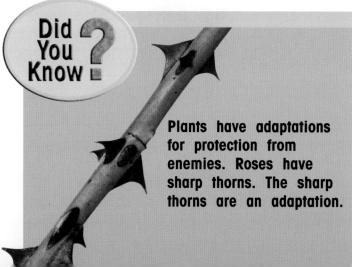

Did You Know?

Plants have adaptations for protection from enemies. Roses have sharp thorns. The sharp thorns are an adaptation.

Adaptations help animals survive.

- Adaptations help animals get food.
- Adaptations protect animals from the weather.
- Adaptations protect animals from enemies.

What Adaptations Help Animals Get Food?

Special body parts help animals get food. Many animals have sharp, strong teeth. The sharp, strong teeth help these animals grab food. The sharp, strong teeth help these animals kill food. The sharp, strong teeth are an adaptation.

▲ Tigers eat other animals.

Tigers have sharp, strong teeth. Tigers use sharp, strong teeth to grab animals. Tigers use sharp, strong teeth to kill animals. The sharp, strong teeth help tigers survive.

Did You Know? Carnivores are animals that eat meat. Carnivores are animals that eat other animals.

Some animals have very good eyes. Good eyes help these animals find food. Good eyes are an adaptation.

▲ Eagles have very good eyes.

Eagles have very good eyes. Good eyes help eagles see their **prey**. Then the eagles catch their prey. Good eyes help eagles survive.

Did You Know ?

Prey are animals other animals eat.

Some animals run very fast. Animals run fast to catch their prey. Running fast is an adaptation. Cheetahs run very fast. Cheetahs run fast to catch their prey. Running fast helps cheetahs survive.

▲ **Cheetahs run fast to catch their food.**

Did You Know?

Chimpanzees use tools to get food. Chimpanzees use sticks to get food. Using sticks is an adaptation.

12

Some animals use **migration** to get food. Migration is moving from place to place. Migration is an adaptation. Wildebeests use migration to get food.

▲ Wildebeests migrate.

Solve This

Wildebeests migrate between 500 and 1,000 miles (804 and 1,608 kilometers) a year. Wildebeests live about 20 years. How many miles do wildebeests migrate in their lifetime?

Answer: 10,000 to 20,000 miles (16,080 to 32,160 kilometers)

Sharks have many adaptations to get food. Sharks have a good sense of smell. Sharks can smell their prey. Sharks have good eyes. Sharks can see prey in dark ocean water.

fast swimming

Sharks can swim fast. Sharks can catch their prey. Sharks have sharp teeth. Sharks can grab their prey.

good sense of smell

good eyes

sharp teeth

Endangered Animals

Sometimes animals cannot get enough food. Giant pandas eat bamboo. The bamboo is disappearing. Giant pandas cannot find enough bamboo to eat.

▲ Giant pandas eat bamboo.

Giant pandas do not eat other types of food. Giant pandas have not made an adaptation. Pandas have not made an adaptation to get new food. Giant pandas are endangered. Endangered means all the pandas might die.

Did You Know?

Sometimes animals must make new adaptations. Animals must make new adaptations to live.

What Adaptations Protect Animals From the Climate?

Some seals live in a cold climate. The seals swim in cold ocean water.

The seals have a thick layer of fat. The fat is blubber. Blubber protects seals from the cold. Blubber is an adaptation.

▲ Seals swim in cold water.

Polar bears live in a cold climate. Polar bears have thick fur. Thick fur protects polar bears from the cold.

Polar bears have blubber. Blubber protects polar bears from the cold. Thick fur and blubber are adaptations.

▲ Polar bears have adaptations for a cold climate.

 Did You Know ?

Polar bears are the largest bears. They can weigh more than 1,750 pounds (794 kilograms).

Many bears live in places with cold winters. The bears cannot find enough food in winter. The bears hibernate all winter. Then the bears do not have to eat.

▲ The bear hibernates.

20

To hibernate is like being asleep.

Camels live in a dry, hot climate. Camels have many adaptations. The adaptations protect camels from the climate.

Fat in the hump keeps the camel alive. The camel uses the fat when there is little food.

Long eyelashes protect the camel's eyes from sand.

It's A Fact

Some camels have one hump. Some camels have two humps.

Nostrils keep the sand out.

Long hair protects the camel from sunburn. The hair keeps the camel warm at night.

The stomach can store enough water for two weeks.

Toes have loose skin between them. The camel does not sink into sand. The skin keeps the camel from sinking.

What Adaptations Protect Animals From Enemies?

Skunks have a bad smell. Other animals stay away from the skunks. Other animals do not eat the skunks. The bad smell protects skunks from their enemies. The bad smell is an adaptation.

▲ Skunks have a bad smell.

Porcupines have quills. Quills are sharp and pointed. The quills protect porcupines from their enemies. The quills are an adaptation.

▲ Porcupines have sharp quills.

Katydids are insects. Katydids look like leaves. Enemies cannot see katydids on the leaves. Looking like leaves protects katydids from their enemies. Looking like leaves is **camouflage**. Camouflage is an adaptation.

▲ This katydid looks like a green leaf.

▲ This katydid looks like a brown and orange leaf.

Walking sticks are insects. Walking sticks look like sticks. Enemies cannot see the walking sticks. Looking like sticks is an adaptation. Looking like sticks is camouflage.

▲ **Walking sticks do not look like insects.**

Try This

Create a butterfly with camouflage:
- Draw and color a habitat for a butterfly.
- Draw and color a butterfly in the habitat.
- Draw and color a butterfly with camouflage.

Chapter 4

Scarlet king snakes are not poisonous. Scarlet king snakes look like coral snakes. Coral snakes are poisonous.

▲ scarlet king snake

Enemies do not attack scarlet king snakes. Enemies think scarlet king snakes are coral snakes. Looking like poisonous snakes is camouflage. Enemies think scarlet king snakes are poisonous.

Figure It Out

Why is looking like a poisonous snake an adaptation?

▲ coral snake

Summary

Adaptations help animals survive. Adaptations help animals get food. Adaptations protect animals from the climate. Adaptations protect animals from their enemies.

Adaptation

What Are Adaptations?

help animals survive

help animals get food

protect animals from the climate

protect animals from enemies

What Adaptations Help Animals Get Food?

strong, sharp teeth

very good eyes

running fast

migration

sense of smell

swimming fast

Think About It

1. What are adaptations?
2. Why are adaptations important?

What Adaptations Protect Animals From the Climate?	What Adaptations Protect Animals From Enemies?
blubber	bad smell
fur	quills
to hibernate	camouflage

Glossary

adaptations things that help animals survive in their habitats

Animals have adaptations to get food.

camouflage animals looking like their surroundings

Katydids have camouflage.

climate weather over a long period of time

Polar bears live in a cold climate.

enemies animals that harm or kill other animals

Animals have enemies.

habitats places where animals and plants live

Adaptations help animals survive in their habitats.

migration moving from place to place

Some animals use migration to get food.

prey animals that other animals eat

*Eagles eat their **prey**.*

protection things that keep animals from being hurt or killed

*Animals have camouflage for **protection**.*

survive live

*Adaptations help animals **survive**.*

Index